W9-ABC-785

I HAVE A QUESTION

I HAVE A QUESTION

72 Fabulously Fun Experiments
You Can Do at Home to Learn the
Science of the World Around Us

CARYL M. LIEBERMAN

Library of Congress Control Number:		2006900158
ISBN 10:	Hardcover	1-4257-0645-2
	Softcover	1-4257-0644-4
ISBN 13:	Hardcover	978-1-4257-0645-6
	Softcover	978-1-4257-0644-9

The publisher and the author have made reasonable efforts to insure that the
experiments and activities in this book are safe when conducted as instructed but
disclaim any liability for any damage caused or sustained while performing the
experiments or activities in this book. Parents, guardians, and/or teachers must
supervise young readers who undertake the experiments and activities in this book.

This book was printed in the United States of America.

To order additional copies of this book, contact:
Xlibris Corporation
1-888-795-4274
www.Xlibris.com
Orders@Xlibris.com
32376

CONTENTS

To the future
Rachel, Jessica, Benjamin, Sarah, and Hannah

INTRODUCTION:
WHAT'S YOUR QUESTION?

Children are natural scientists. Loaded with questions, curious about . . . everything. And I love questions. Science begins—and ends—with questions. Such as: How does a thermometer work? How do clouds make rain? Why can I lift my big brother in a swimming pool? What is sound? What's in a rainbow?

This book will teach you the scientific principles behind the way things work. Its experiments—organized into the following five sections—Heat, Water, Air, Light and Color, and Sound—are fabulously fun. They are rated in levels of 1, 2, and 3, from simple to complicated. Thousands of my students have enjoyed the *Aha!* moments these experiments reveal. I hope you will, too.

Caryl Lieberman

THE HEAT IS ON

Heat is a form of energy. It is invisible, like the air. It can be measured, yet it can't be caught. From a gentle breeze to a powerful explosion, energy makes things happen.

Heat can travel. Not by plane or spaceship, but through our atmosphere. The most obvious example is the light rays that travel from the sun to warm up our planet Earth. By moving from molecule to molecule, heat makes the wind blow and water boil. But did you also know that as molecules move faster and faster, they begin to glow? They give off light. The flame of a candle glows when particles of carbon from the melting wax have been made white-hot. In a lightbulb, the wire, or filament, inside the bulb becomes so hot with electricity that it glows. If you have an electric space heater at home, turn it on and watch the metal coils glow as they heat up.

By doing the experiments that follow, you'll learn how a thermometer works, how heat travels, what the domino effect is, and why wearing that cool black outfit on a summer day doesn't make you feel cool at all.

WHY DOES THE WIND BLOW?

Heat energy makes things move. It can move water molecules around faster and faster until the water comes to a boil. It can circulate through air and create an air current. Let's explore the different things that cause the wind to blow.

Creating Convection

ADULT HELP REQUIRED   LEVEL: 1

Make a miniature volcano to learn how molecules move when they are heated.
You will need:
large glass bowl
small empty baby food jar
cold water and hot (not scalding) water
food coloring, any color

1. Fill the bowl with cold water. Fill the baby food jar with hot water.
2. Put two or three drops of food coloring into the hot water in the baby food jar. This makes it easier to tell the hot water from the cold water.
3. Submerge the baby food jar (mouth up) in the bowl.

What happens?
The colored water moves up and out of the baby food jar, then down, then swirls around in the bowl, like the eruption of a volcano.

Why?

All things, whether they are solid, liquid, or gas, are made of molecules. A molecule is the smallest bit of a substance that still has the properties of that substance. The pages of this book are made up of molecules. You yourself are made up of molecules. These molecules are always moving, even though the object itself doesn't look like it's moving. When you heated the water in this experiment, the molecules in the water moved faster. As they speed up, they bump into each other. This gives them more energy, and they move farther and farther apart. They take up more space.

A fluid is a substance that can easily change its shape. All gases and liquids are fluids. Water is a fluid. Air, a gas, is a fluid. Wind is air that is moving. When air is heated, the molecules closest to the source of heat speed up, collide, and spread farther apart. The hot molecules become lighter and rise above the colder molecules. Colder, denser air comes in to take its place. This process is called *convection*.

So, why *does* the wind blow?

As the sun heats the earth, the air gets warmer and becomes lighter. The warmer air moves up, and cold air moves down to where the warm air was. This movement forms the wind.

Balloon Blast

ADULT HELP REQUIRED   LEVEL: 2

Here's a trick that's just full of hot air . . . but in a good way.

You will need:
small balloon
empty 1- or 2-liter soda bottle
rubber band
bowl of hot (not scalding) water

1. First, stretch out the balloon by blowing it up and letting the air out.
2. Stretch the mouth of the balloon over the neck of the bottle. Make sure it fits securely. Use the rubber band to hold it in place.
3. Hold the bottle and the attached balloon in the bowl of hot water. Hold it firmly so that the bottom of the bottle sits on the bottom of the bowl. Watch what happens. (It may take a little while for the bottle to heat up. Be patient.)

What happens?
The balloon fills with air and inflates.

Why?
As you learned in Creating Convection (page 14), air expands when it is heated. The hot water in the bowl heated up the air inside the bottle. As the air expanded, it needed to go somewhere. The heated air entered the balloon and began filling it up, causing it to inflate.

In a Lot of Hot Water

ADULT HELP REQUIRED   LEVEL: 2

Here's another demonstration of how water molecules move. Fill a coffee pot about halfway with water. Place the pot on the stove on high heat. As you watch the water come to a boil, answer the following questions. What do you see forming? Where do they form? How do they move? Where do they go?

Make a Spinner

LEVEL: 3

If air is invisible, how do we know that air molecules really move? This experiment will help show you how.

You will need:
sheet of plain white paper
scissors
ruler
sharp pencil
string

1. Cut out a square at least 8 x 8 inches (20 x 20 cm) from the sheet of paper.
2. Now, make a spiral out of the square. Starting at the outer edge, cut in a circular motion, working toward the middle of the square (see illustration). Do not cut out the center.
3. Poke a small hole in the center of the spiral with the pencil point.
4. Cut a piece of string about 12 inches (30 cm) long. Thread the string through the hole. Tie a big knot in one end so that the string will not slip out.
5. Hold your spiral over something that gives off heat, such as a bright lamp or a radiator.

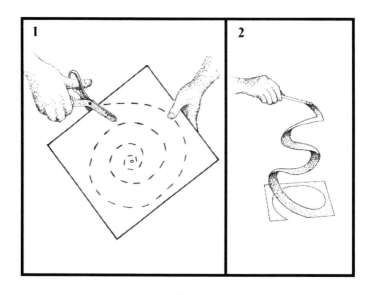

What happens?
The paper spiral begins to spin.

Why?
When air heats up, its molecules move faster. The air molecules bumped into the spiral and began pushing it, making it spin.

Try This!

Hold the spiral over something even warmer. Does it spin faster?

Breaking Up Isn't Hard to Do

ADULT HELP REQUIRED   LEVEL: 1

Which will a sugar cube dissolve faster in—hot water or cold? And if you already know the answer, do you know *why?*

You will need:
glass measuring cup
hot (not scalding) water and cold water
2 drinking glasses
2 sugar cubes
magnifying glass

1. Measure and pour 1/2 cup hot water into one glass and 1/2 cup cold water into the other glass.
2. At exactly the same time, drop a sugar cube into each glass.
3. Watch what happens using the magnifying glass.

What happens?
The sugar cube that was dropped into the hot water starts to break up and dissolve first.

Why?
Heat energy causes water molecules to move faster. As they scoot around, they bump into the sugar cube at a more rapid rate than the slower-moving cold-water molecules. This makes the sugar cube in the hot water dissolve more quickly.

The Big Mix-Up

ADULT HELP REQUIRED   LEVEL: 1

Put 1/2 cup of hot (not scalding) water into a clear container, and 1/2 cup of cold water into a second container. Hold an eyedropperful of food coloring over each container. Squeeze one drop of food coloring into each container at the same time. In which container does the color mix more quickly?

HOW DOES A THERMOMETER WORK?

An outdoor thermometer tells you how hot it is outside—or how cold. And when you're sick, you put an oral thermometer in your mouth to find out whether you have a fever. How does the liquid inside a thermometer measure heat and cold? The following experiments will help you understand.

Temperatures Rising

ADULT HELP REQUIRED   LEVEL: 2

By making a thermometer out of straw and clay, you'll learn how heat makes substances grow bigger.

You will need:
tall, empty glass jar (such as an olive jar)
water
food coloring, any color
clear drinking straw
modeling clay
felt-tip marker
bowl deep enough to fit the olive jar inside

1. Fill the jar almost to the top with water. Add a few drops of food coloring.
2. Place the straw in the jar. Use a piece of clay to form a stopper at the top of the straw.
3. Press gently on the clay until the water rises about an inch inside the straw. Mark the water level with the felt-tip marker.
4. Fill the bowl with hot (not scalding) water. Stand the jar and straw in the bowl of hot water.

What happens?
The liquid begins climbing even higher inside the straw.

Why?
As you've learned, heat makes most things grow bigger, or expand. Most thermometers (the non-digital kind) have a thin column of liquid, called mercury, or colored alcohol, inside a sealed glass tube. When the mercury gets hot from the sun (as in an outdoor thermometer), or from being inside your mouth (as in an oral thermometer), it expands. It has no other way to go than UP. When heat is lost, the liquid shrinks, or contracts. This causes the liquid to move DOWN.

Down to the Wire

ADULT HELP REQUIRED   LEVEL: 3

See how heat affects other materials besides liquid and air.

You will need:
ruler
picture-hanging wire (or other uninsulated wire)
chair with an open back (one you can tie something to)
screwdriver
wire cutters or scissors
candle and matches

1. Measure a length of wire roughly from the top of the chair back to just above the floor.
2. Tie one end of the wire to the blade of the screwdriver.
3. Tie the other end of the wire to the back of the chair and let the screwdriver hang down. The bottom of the screwdriver should hang just under the bottom rung of the chair. If the chair doesn't have rungs, the screwdriver bottom should hang about 6 inches (15 cm) from the floor. Trim the wire as needed.
4. Light the candle. Heat the midpoint of the wire with the candle.

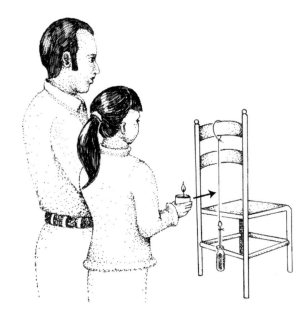

What happens?
The screwdriver drops lower.

Why?
Heat also makes the molecules in solid objects, such as metals, move faster. Metal conducts heat. The picture wire, being metal, expanded when it was heated, causing the screwdriver to drop. What do you think will happen when the wire cools off? Will the screwdriver be pulled back up? (Remember, most materials contract, or shrink, when they cool off.)

Did You Know?

Architects and builders know that heat energy makes most materials expand. That's why bridges are built with expansion joints, and railroad tracks have gaps in between. This leaves room for the joints and the tracks to expand on a hot day. Otherwise, the metal would have no room to expand, and the tracks would buckle and bend. A ride on a train might end up like a ride on a roller coaster!

Concrete, used to make buildings, sidewalks, roads, freeway overpasses, and other structures, also expands when it is heated. That's why sidewalks and roads are built with spaces between sections. If there is no room for expansion, sidewalks and roads can buckle and crack.

What Do You Think?

You need to open a brand-new jar of spaghetti sauce. The metal top is on tight. You look for a jar opener but can't find one. You know that heat makes metals expand, but you are not allowed to turn on the stove. How would you open that jar in a safe, but scientific, way?

That's right! Run the jar under hot water in the sink. This should help make the metal lid expand and loosen enough so you can get it off.

WHY DO WE WEAR LIGHT-COLORED CLOTHING IN THE SUMMERTIME?

The sun warms the earth, but not every area heats up at the same rate. Let's find out how color affects temperature.

Black and White

LEVEL: 2

Ever notice that you feel warmer when you wear dark-colored clothes on a sunny day? This experiment will help explain why.

You will need:
newspapers
black paint and white paint
paintbrush
2 small, empty, clean cans (such as tuna cans)
glue
2 pennies

1. Lay newspapers over your work area.
2. Paint the outside of one can black and the other can white.
3. Put a drop or two of glue on each penny. Stick a penny on the bottom of the inside of each can. Let dry.
4. Turn the cans upside down. Place them on a sunny windowsill or under a lighted desk lamp (make sure the lightbulb gives off a lot of heat). Listen closely.

What happens?
Eventually you will hear the pennies drop. The penny that was glued to the can painted black should drop first.

Why?
Besides convection, another way heat travels is through *radiation*. We feel this type of energy every day. It comes from the sun. Invisible waves of radiation, called *infrared*, travel through empty space. When this energy is absorbed by an object—in this case, the two cans—the molecules of that object begin to move faster and become hotter. The can that was

painted black absorbed more radiation than the white can did. It became hotter first. Because of this, the glue melted more quickly and the penny dropped off first.

So, why *do* we wear light-colored clothing in summer?

Some colors absorb radiation better others. White tends to *reflect*, or bounce away, radiation. Black tends to *absorb*, or take in, radiation. The radiation itself is not heat, but it becomes heat when it is absorbed. Because black absorbs more radiation, dark-colored clothes, in general, would make you hotter.

The Great American Melt-Off

LEVEL: 1

How well do other colors absorb radiation? Gather five sheets of construction paper, one in each of these colors: white, black, red, green, and blue. Get five ice cubes out of the freezer and place one ice cube on each sheet. Arrange the sheets outdoors in a sunny spot. How long does it take for each ice cube to melt? Do some colors absorb more radiation than other colors? Which ones?

Did You Know?

You may have seen rows of flat panels arranged at an angle on the roof of a building. These are used for solar heating. A solar heater traps the intense heat of the sun and uses it to heat water. It consists of panels, metal tubes, and a storage tank. Cool water runs through these metal tubes. The solar panels absorb heat, which is carried through the metal tubes. As the metal gets hot, it heats the water inside. The hot water is then stored in the storage tank. Solar heating is an alternate source of heat. It is used in addition to or in place of heat created with electricity or gas.

HOW DOES HEAT MOVE?

You've learned that heat causes something to warm up by making its molecules move faster. But can heat itself move from one object to another?

Penny-wise

LEVEL: 2

This experiment demonstrates how heat travels from warmer objects to cooler objects.

You will need:
ice cube
small bowl
penny

1. Place the ice cube in the bowl, with the flattest side of the ice cube facing up.
2. Put the penny on top of the ice cube.
3. With your finger, push as hard as you can on the penny. Note what happens. Now take your finger away and wait a few minutes.

What happens?

The penny is pushed into the ice cube as the ice cube starts to melt. When you take your finger away, the melted water eventually freezes around the penny.

Why?

Heat travels from warmer objects to cooler objects. Your finger has the most heat, the penny has less heat, and the ice cube even less. In this experiment, the heat from your finger flowed into the penny, and then from the penny into the ice cube. Enough energy transferred so that the penny was pushed into the ice cube. Once you removed the heat source by taking away your finger, the melted water refroze over the penny.

One way that heat moves is by passing from one molecule to another, called *conduction*. When heat is conducted, the molecules closest to the source of the heat (your finger) move faster. These faster-moving molecules then bump into those near them (the penny) and cause them to move faster, until the substance becomes warm. Once that happens, the heat continues to pass into the object nearest it (the ice cube).

Try This!

What would happen if you did not push on the penny? The penny would still melt the ice, but at a slower rate. The penny is not as warm as your finger, but it is warmer than the ice cube. Remember, heat always moves from warmer objects into cooler ones.

Did You Know?

At the beach on a hot summer's day, have you ever walked on the sand without shoes or sandals on? OUCH! The sun makes the sand hot. When you walk on the sand, conduction causes the heat to move into your bare feet.

Soup's On!

LEVEL: 1

The next time you have a bowl of soup that is too hot to eat, try this. Place your metal spoon in the bowl of soup. As the soup cools, the spoon warms up. In a few minutes, the soup will be just right. Most metals are good conductors of heat. How well do you think a plastic spoon would work? Not well, because plastic is a poor conductor of heat.

Did You Know?

When you enjoy a dish of ice cream, you are helping to make the room cooler. How? The heat from the room flows into the ice cream and melts it, releasing cold air molecules.

The Domino Effect

LEVEL: 1

You may have done this before, or seen it done on TV. Hundreds of dominoes are lined up, often in fancy, carefully designed patterns. The first one is tipped over, causing the remaining dominoes to fall in succession. It's a demonstration of how conduction works.

You will need:
at least 10 dominoes

1. Work on a large tabletop or on a bare floor (not carpeted). Set up the dominos in a row. Stand them on end, with about a half inch of space in between each.
2. Tap the first domino toward the others.

What happens?
When the first domino is tipped over, it knocks down the one next to it, which knocks down the next one, and so on.

Why?
Let's pretend the dominos are molecules. Your finger is a source of heat. When you tap the first domino—the molecule closest to the source of heat—it moves faster. This molecule bumps into the next one, causing that one to move faster, and so on. As heat is conducted from one molecule (domino) to the next, the substance becomes hotter and hotter.

Did You Know?

The annual domino challenge known as Domino Day has been held in the Netherlands since 1986. In 2004, nearly 4 million dominoes (3,992,397, to be exact) were toppled over, setting a new team world record.

Did You Know?

When one event sets off a sequence of events, or chain reaction, that's called the *domino effect*. Let's say a car engine overheats. This leads to more fuel being used up, then more engine oil. This affects the spark plugs, and eventually the entire engine will break down.

On a much larger scale, researchers believe the slaughter of more than half a million great whales in the Pacific Ocean, starting in 1949, set off a disastrous domino effect that is still unfolding to this day. Killer whales—which feed on great whales—were forced to start hunting smaller marine mammals. This led to a rapid decline in the population of seals, sea lions, and sea otters. In turn, sea urchins—which otters like to eat—have grown in number and begun damaging the kelp beds along the Alaskan coast.

I'm Melting . . . !

ADULT HELP REQUIRED   LEVEL: 3

If you placed three blobs of wax on a coat hanger and heated one end of the hanger, which blob would melt first? Or would they all melt at the same time?

You will need:
wire hanger
ruler and chalk
matches
brightly colored birthday-cake candle
large candle
potholder

1. Ask an adult to help you untwist and straighten out the hanger (it doesn't have to be completely straightened out).
2. Measure and mark off with the chalk 1 1/2, 2 1/2, and 3 1/2 inches (4, 6, and 9 cm) from one end of the wire hanger.
3. Light the birthday candle. Drip two blobs of wax on each marked-off spot on the hanger.
4. Light the large candle. Use a potholder to hold the hanger in one hand. With your other hand (or have a grown-up do this), hold the candle flame at the end of the hanger closest to the wax blobs.

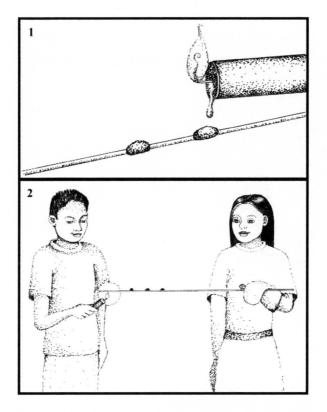

What happens?

As the heat is conducted along the hanger, the wax blob closest to the source of heat melts first. The second closest melts next, then the third.

Why?

In conduction, heat passes through an object or substance. In other words, the object doesn't heat up all at once, but gradually as the heat moves through.

WATER, WATER, EVERYWHERE

All of the water that is on the earth today has been here since the beginning of time. We are drinking the same water that the dinosaurs drank! And we are not likely to get a new shipment of water from outer space anytime soon, so we must conserve and recycle what we have.

Water has unique properties that sustain life on earth. There is water in the cells of all living things, including you. It is a wonderfully effective solvent, and it can dissolve at least small amounts of almost *anything...* even rock!

This precious resource moves continuously through a never-ending cycle. Water in the ocean evaporates into the air. Water vapor condenses into clouds and then returns back to earth through *precipitation* (pree-sip-ih-TAY-shun), or rain. The rain collects in lakes, rivers, and underground rocks that are *porous* (PORE-us), or full of small openings. Finally, it flows into the ocean, where the cycle begins all over again. The experiments in this section will explore how the various parts of this cycle work.

WHERE DOES THE WATER GO WHEN A PUDDLE DRIES UP?

This experiment illustrates one part of the water cycle.

Disappearing Act

LEVEL: 2

Now you see the water, now you don't. But is it really gone?

You will need:
Glass or plastic measuring cup
water
2 small, clear glasses, such as juice glasses
plastic wrap
rubber band
marker

1. Pour 2 ounces of water into each glass.
2. Cover one of the glasses with plastic wrap. Secure with the rubber band. Leave the other glass uncovered.
3. Mark the water level on each glass with the washable marker.
4. Wait 2 to 3 days. Observe the water levels.

What happens?
The water in the uncovered glass seems to have disappeared. The water in the covered glass is still there.

Why?
Water wears three different hats. It can be a solid, a liquid, or a gas. The water that we drink and that we use to wash with is a liquid. The water in the ice cubes we use to make drinks cold, and the ice on which we skate, is a solid. We can see liquid and solid water. But like air, water can be invisible, too. This form is called water vapor, and it is a gas.

The water in the uncovered glass did not go away. You just can't see it anymore because it changed into invisible water vapor. The water has *evaporated*. The plastic wrap over the covered glass keeps the water from escaping into the air.

What Do You Think?

What would happen if you put 2 ounces of water in a container shaped like an olive jar (tall and thin)?

And 2 ounces of water in a container shaped like a baking pan (short and wide)?

From which container would the water evaporate first?

Water—and all liquids, for that matter—evaporates from the surface. The larger the surface area, the faster the rate of evaporation. That's why the water in the wide container would evaporate first. Moving air (wind) and heat also speed up evaporation.

Hiding in Plain Sight

LEVEL: 1

How can you make water evaporate faster? Using water as your paint, paint a picture on a sheet of plain white paper or outdoors on the sidewalk. Watch what happens after you stop painting. Your picture vanishes.

Now paint two pictures on two new sheets of paper or on the sidewalk again. Try to make them the same, using the same amount of water on your paintbrush. Fold another sheet of paper into a fan. Fan one of the pictures. Does this picture evaporate first?

We're Just Getting Warmed Up

LEVEL: 1

Here's another way to explore the different conditions under which water will evaporate. Get two small drinking glasses. Put 2 ounces of water into each glass. Place one of the glasses in a warm spot, such as under a lighted desk lamp or next to a radiator. Put the other glass in another spot that is at room temperature, such as on your desk or a countertop, or anyplace that is not in direct sunlight. From which cup will the water evaporate first?

Fire and Ice

ADULT HELP SUGGESTED   LEVEL: 1

Place an ice cube in a bowl. Watch as it melts. Will the melted water evaporate as well? Can you speed up the process by putting the ice cube in a pot instead of a bowl and heating it on the stove?

Why?

If you said "yes" both times, you were right on the mark. The molecules of all substances (solids, liquids, gases) are always moving. The higher the temperature, the more rapid the motion. As the temperature rises, the molecules move faster and faster, escape from the surface of the water more quickly, and become invisible water vapor. In other words, heating the pot makes the water disappear faster.

HOW CAN WE MAKE THE EVAPORATED WATER COME BACK?

When you go outdoors in the early morning, have you seen drops of water or moisture on your bicycle, or on your parents' car? Those drops are formed by *condensation*. It's the opposite of evaporation. The following experiments will help you understand how condensation works.

"Can" Do

LEVEL: 3

You can't see it, but water is in the air all around you as water vapor. Use this experiment to make that water visible.

You will need:
clean, empty, shiny can, label removed
glass measuring cup
water
ice cubes
food coloring, any color
magnifying glass
white paper towel

1. Carefully observe and run your fingers over the outside of the can. Remember how it feels. Make notes if you wish.
2. Pour about 2 ounces of water into the can.
3. Carefully add a few ice cubes to the can. Don't splash any water onto the outside of the can.
4. Add two or three drops of food coloring to the water.
5. Wait a few minutes. Look at the can through the magnifying glass. Feel the outside of the can again. Does it feel different? If so, how is it different?
6. Using the paper towel, wipe the moisture off the outside of the can. Look at the paper towel. Is it still white?

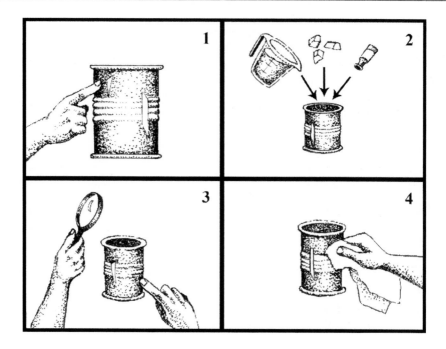

What happens?

Water droplets form on the outside of the can. After wiping the can, the paper towel is damp, but still white.

Why?

The ice cubes made the metal of the can cold. When air touched the cold metal, the temperature of the air also became cold. This caused the water vapor that was in the air to change to liquid. This water formed on the outside of the can. That's why the can feels wet. The water *condensed*.

If the condensed water had come from the water *inside* the can, the moisture that formed on the outside of the can would have been the color of the food coloring. The color would have appeared on the paper towel when you wiped the outside of the can.

Seeing Is Believing

LEVEL: 2

This setup is similar to that of Disappearing Act (page 38), but the result illustrates both condensation *and* evaporation. "See" for yourself.

You will need:
glass measuring cup
water
small, clear glass
plastic wrap
rubber band
grease pencil

1. Put 2 ounces of water into the glass.
2. Cover the glass securely with the plastic wrap. Hold it in place with the rubber band.
3. Mark the water level with the grease pencil.
4. Place the glass on a sunny windowsill or under a bright desk lamp.
5. Wait a day. Look at the plastic wrap. What do you see on the underside of the wrap? Is the water level in the glass the same?

What happens?
You should see droplets of moisture on the underside of the wrap. The water level should be slightly lower than when you started.

Why?
First, heat causes some of the water to dry up, or evaporate. It changes into vapor and rises up, but the wrap keeps it from escaping. When the water vapor touches the cool plastic wrap, it condenses and changes back to liquid.

Try This!

Next time you take a hot shower, look at the bathroom mirror after you're done. What do you see? How long does it last? Do you know where it came from, and where it goes?

And, the next time the weather is very cold, go out for a walk. Open your mouth and exhale. What do you see coming out of your mouth?

Did You Know?

Have you ever wondered what makes popcorn pop? Inside each kernel of unpopped corn is a little moisture. When the kernels are heated, this water changes from liquid to gas. In doing so, it takes up more space. As the gas expands, the kernel pops.

WHY DOES IT RAIN?

We all know how to describe it: the air gets damp, the clouds grow dark and gray, and then the rain comes down. But what exactly causes rain, and where does all that water come from?

Sticking Together

LEVEL: 1

Like birds of a feather, drops of water stick together, too. It's called *cohesion.*

You will need:
cup of water
medicine dropper or straw
square of waxed paper, at least 5 x 5 inches (13 x 13 cm)
toothpick or pencil

1. Draw water into the medicine dropper. Scatter several drops of water on the square of waxed paper.
2. Use the toothpick to move the drops of water around. Observe as much as you can about the drops of water:

   - Can you get a drop to follow your toothpick?
   - Can you make a drop snap back like a rubber band?
   - What happens when you make a drop touch another drop?
   - Can you break a large drop into smaller ones?
   - Can you blow the drops across the paper?

What happens?
The drops of water follow your toothpick. When two drops touch, they become one. You can also break up a large drop into smaller drops.

Why?
Water forms into drops because each molecule of water attracts its neighboring molecules. The force of attraction that makes water stick together is called *cohesion* (koh-HEE-zhun).

So, why *does* it rain?

Let's go back to the water cycle. We'll start with a drop of water in the ocean. The sun's heat makes that drop evaporate by changing it from a liquid to a gas. Thousands upon thousands of drops evaporate and climb up into the air. *Condensation* (see Seeing Is Believing, page 45) causes the drops of water vapor to gather around tiny dust particles in the air to form a cloud. The drops move around within the cloud. They bump into each other and stick together through cohesion. As more drops stick together, they form larger and larger masses. Eventually they become so heavy that gravity pulls them down as rain.

Make Your Own Rain Cloud

ADULT HELP REQUIRED   LEVEL: 2

To give you a better idea of the principle you learned in Sticking Together (page 47), let's make a miniature rain cloud.

You will need:
ice cubes
clean glass jar
glass measuring cup
hot (not scalding) water
bright lamp or flashlight

1. You should have enough ice cubes to cover the mouth of the jar. Make one big ice cube by squeezing some small ice cubes together. They will melt and refreeze into a large ice cube.
2. Pour 8 ounces of hot water into the jar. Place the large ice cube over the mouth. Put the jar under the bright lamp, or shine the flashlight on it. Wait and watch what happens.

What happens?
The melting ice "rains" into the jar.

Why?

Water evaporates from the surface of the warm water in the jar. This water vapor rises and meets the cool air beneath the ice cube. As the water vapor is cooled, it changes back (and condenses) into water droplets. The droplets meet, stick together (cohesion), get larger and heavier, and finally fall as rain.

Things Are Getting Tense

LEVEL: 2

How many drops of water can you put on a penny before the water overflows? It's more than you think! And while you're at it, you'll learn about surface tension and cohesion, too.

You will need:
penny
paper towel
pencil and paper
cup of water
medicine dropper

1. Place the penny on the paper towel.
2. Predict (guess) how many drops of water you can get on the penny before the water overflows. Record the number.
3. Draw water into the medicine dropper. Count each drop as you begin carefully dropping water on the surface of the penny. Continue adding until the water overflows.
4. How many drops did you use? Record the number.
5. Which side of the penny did you use, heads or tails? Wipe the penny dry and repeat steps 1 through 4, using the OTHER side. Did it make a difference which side you used?

What happens?
You'll be surprised at how many drops of water will fit. The number probably was higher than you predicted. (Our record was 56.) If you bend down to get an eye-level view of the water on the penny, you'll see that it's not flat, but shaped like a half dome.

Why?

Cohesion makes water molecules stick to each other. They stick so tightly that they form an invisible skin in a *convex* shape (bulging outward). This skin is called *surface tension*.

Try This!

Do the above experiment again, first using a dime and then a quarter. Are you able to fit the same number of drops on each type of coin? More drops? Fewer drops? Why do you think this is so?

The Rules of Attraction

LEVEL: 2

Let's take the water-on-a-penny idea a step further. How many pennies can you put into a glass of water before it overflows?

You will need:
small, clear drinking glass
water
handful of pennies
pencil and paper

1. Fill the glass to the rim with water.
2. Carefully drop in the pennies, one by one, keeping count. Observe what happens to the water level as you add the coins. Stop when the water is just about to overflow out of the glass.
3. How many pennies did you add? Record the number, then draw the shape of the water bulging at the top of the glass.
4. Spill out just a little of the water. Note the surface of the water now. Draw it on your paper.

What happens?
As you add each penny, the water level rises higher and higher above the top of the glass instead of spilling out. The water surface seems to bulge outward and upward. Surprisingly, many pennies can be added before the water spills over.

When you tip a little water out of the glass, the surface of the water curves inward. The water seems to rise slightly above the glass, as if it were being pulled by an invisible force.

Why?
What makes the water bulge instead of spilling out? It's cohesion. The water molecules cling to each other to keep from separating. This creates the convex bulge shape at the top of the glass.

When you spilled out some of the water, the surface of the water became *concave* (curved inward). The water rises a bit around the outer edge. The water seems to be clinging to the glass. This is called *adhesion* (ad-HEE-zhun). The molecules in water and in glass attract each other. The glass molecules pulled up the water molecules around the edges to form a concave surface.

Dirty Work

LEVEL: 3

In this experiment, you'll see how surface tension works, and how to make it stop working.

You will need:
soup bowl
water
paper clip
plastic fork
liquid soap or liquid dishwashing detergent

1. Fill the soup bowl with water. Hang the paper clip on one of the tines on the plastic fork.
2. Holding the fork, carefully lower the paper clip onto the surface of the water in the soup bowl. Practice until you can make the paper clip float. Why do you think it floats?
3. Now put a drop of soap on your fingertip. Dip your finger in the water.

What happens?
The paper clip floats because of surface tension. As you learned in the previous experiment, when water molecules stick together, they form a skin. This skin holds up the paper clip. When you put your soapy finger in the water, the paper clip sinks.

Why?
The soap broke the elastic skin on the water. That's why we use soap to make us clean. It breaks the surface tension of the water so that the soap can clean the dirt off your hands and body.

Everything That Rises

LEVEL: 1

A floating object always moves to the highest position possible. Fill a glass with enough water so that it forms a convex surface *above* the rim of the glass. The highest point in this convex surface is at the center. Place a small cork or piece of cork in the center. It should stay right in the center. Try placing it away from the center and see what happens. (Instead of cork, you can use small paper circles punched out with a hole puncher.) Tip some water out of the glass. The water surface becomes concave, and the center is now the lowest point. If you put the cork in, it will float away from the center to the outer edge, where the surface of the water is higher.

CAN WATER CLIMB UPHILL?

We all know that rain comes down, and that waterfalls fall down. But did you know that water can climb *up*, defying gravity? Perform these experiments and find out how!

Narrowing Things Down

LEVEL: 1

Allow us to introduce two forces of nature. Adhesion, meet cohesion. Together, they create *capillarity*.

You will need:
glass
water
food coloring, any color
clear drinking straw

1. Fill the glass halfway with water. Add a few drops of food coloring.
2. Place the straw in the glass of water. Look at the water level in the straw.

What happens?
The level of the water inside the straw is higher than the level of the water in the glass.

Why?
When water rises inside a narrow space or tube, it is called *capillarity* (kap-ih-LAIR-ih-tee). It is caused by two forces working together. One force, *adhesion*, attracts water molecules to the molecules in glass, paper, wood, and other non-water substances. The other force, *cohesion*, attracts water molecules to other water molecules, helping to hold the water together.

When a tube with a narrow opening, such as a straw, is placed in a liquid, such as water, the molecules in the water are attracted to the molecules in the straw. This attraction is stronger than the attraction of water molecules for each other. Because of this, the water is pulled up into the straw. The water climbs until the forces of adhesion and cohesion that pull the water up the straw are equal to the force of gravity that pulls the water down. Then the water stops. Because of capillarity, water can climb up through narrow roots all the way to the top of a tree.

Faster and Slower

LEVEL: 1

Place three straws of different widths in a bowl of water. Does the water in all the straws rise above the water level? Does it rise higher in some than in others? The water will rise highest in the narrowest straw. The wider the straw, the stronger the force of gravity, preventing capillarity from pulling the water up.

Side by Side

LEVEL: 1

Put two straight-sided drinking glasses in a tray or shallow pan of colored water. Bring the sides of the two glasses as close together as you can without touching. Watch what happens to the water level in the narrow space between the glasses.

Drink Up!

ADULT HELP REQUIRED   LEVEL: 2

You know that plants take in water through their roots, but you probably haven't seen *how* they do it.

You will need:
tall glass
water
red food coloring
knife
celery stalk

1. Fill the glass about three-quarters full of water. Add a few drops of food coloring.
2. Cut the bottom end off the stalk of celery.
3. Stand the celery, cut side down, in the glass of water. Wait 2 hours.
4. Remove the celery and cut across the stalk horizontally. Look inside. What do you see?

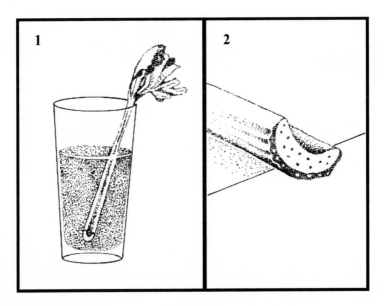

What happens?
You should see tiny red dots where you cut the celery. The red is the colored water that climbed up into the stalk.

Why?

Capillarity (see Narrowing Things Down, page 56) caused the water to be drawn up into the stalk. Adhesion attracted the water to the celery stalk, and cohesion helped the water molecules stay together.

If you cut the celery stalk vertically, you'll see that each red dot is really a tube that carries the water upward, just like when you drink through a straw!

It's a Wrap!

LEVEL: 2

Here's a similar demonstration of how plants drink up water.

You will need:
wrapped drinking straw
medicine dropper
water

1. Tear off one end of the wrapper. Slowly and carefully push down the wrapper around the straw.
2. Remove the wrapper and place it on a flat surface. You should have an accordion-like "snake." Place a few drops of water on the wrapper.

What happens?
The "snake" uncoils right before your eyes.

Why?
Paper is made up of plant fibers. These fibers are composed of tiny tubes. The water is pulled into these tubes by capillarity. As they take in water, the tubes start to expand, and the paper "snake" uncoils.

Flower Power

ADULT HELP REQUIRED   LEVEL: 3

Fill two tall glasses with water. Color one glass of water with red food coloring and the other with blue food coloring. Put the glasses side by side. With a knife, make a vertical cut from the bottom of the carnation stem to about halfway up. Pull the two stem halves apart slightly. Place one half in each glass as shown. Wait 2 to 3 hours. What has happened to the flower?

Water on the Move

LEVEL: 2

Can you empty a glass of water without pouring it out? Place two glasses 6 inches apart. Fill one of the glasses halfway with water. Place this glass on a thick book so that it is higher than the other glass. Twist or roll up a paper towel and place one end in each glass. Wait 5 to 6 hours. Most, if not all, of the water will have transferred to the other glass.

WHY DON'T FISH FREEZE IN FROZEN LAKES AND PONDS?

If a lake, pond, or river freezes over in the winter, it would seem to follow that the fish, plants, and any other living things below would freeze too. But they don't. Why not?

The Ice Is Right

LEVEL: 1

Remember, water wears three hats. It exists as a solid, a liquid, and a gas. It can change its form by freezing and melting, and through evaporation and condensation. It is also one of the few substances that expands when it freezes.

You will need:
empty 1-liter soda bottle, label removed
water
felt-tip marker
freezer

1. Pour water into the soda bottle until it is about half full. Place the bottle on a level surface and wait until the water stops moving.
2. Bend down so that you are eye level with the surface of the water in the bottle. Mark the water level with the marker.
3. Put the bottle in the freezer and leave it overnight.
4. The next day, check the water level. What do you notice about it?

What happens?
The liquid water has changed to solid ice, but the level of the ice is *higher* than the mark you made with the marker.

Why?
Unlike most substances, water expands as it freezes. Because of this, ice is lighter than liquid water. When you put ice cubes in a drink, they bob for a while, then settle at the top and stay afloat.

The same goes for ice in frozen lakes and rivers. It settles at the top, so only the top of the water actually freezes. The water beneath remains liquid. The ice acts as a shield that protects the living creatures below the surface. If ice were heavier than water, the bottom of the lake would fill with ice, and the entire lake would freeze, along with any plants or animals.

Did You Know?

Seventy percent of your body weight is made up of water. The water in your body helps dissolve the food you eat. Nutrients from the food are then carried by your blood (which is almost all water) to every part of your body. Water carries away the wastes from your cells. It also helps to keep your body at the right temperature.

If the amount of water in your body changes, you feel the difference. If it drops a little, you feel thirsty. If it drops a lot, it is dangerous to your health. You can live without food for several weeks, but you cannot live for longer than a week without water.

THE AIR UP THERE

It's not an exaggeration to say that we—and the entire Earth, for that matter—are constantly surrounded by a blanket of air, or *atmosphere*. Air is all around us, and so is *air pressure*. Air pressure is air pushing against something. Air is pushing on us all the time from all sides. We don't feel it because it pushes on us evenly from all directions. What keeps us from getting squashed? Our bodies! Each of the cells that make up our bodies is like a balloon, pushing back against air pressure so we don't end up looking like a pancake.

The closer you are to the ground, the greater the air pressure. As you move higher into the sky (the atmosphere), increasing your *altitude*, the air pressure decreases. At the top of a mountain, air pressure is lower. If you move even higher, into outer space, there is no air pressure because there is no atmosphere. Your body cells would still be pushing outward, but there would be no outside air pressure to counter it, and you would explode. That's why astronauts wear spacesuits. The suits contain air for them to breathe, and also keep this air at the right pressure to push against their bodies.

Although it is invisible, air is a real force. It even protects us from objects that come from outer space. Earth's atmosphere acts as an invisible shield against small bits of matter called *meteors*. When these small chunks of matter reach our atmosphere, they are moving extremely fast. As they move, they push against the air, causing *friction*. (As an example, rub the palms of your hands together very fast. Now do it faster! What do you feel? Heat!) Friction creates intense heat that often burns up the meteors, producing *shooting stars*. Meteors that make it to the earth's surface in larger forms are called *meteorites*.

CAN AIR STOP A SPILL?

You can't see air and, most of the time, you can't feel it. But you can move through it on a bicycle, in a car, or on an airplane. Air can be lighter than a feather, but strong enough to hold back water. The following experiments will show you how.

It's in the Cards

LEVEL: 2

Note: Do this experiment over a sink—just in case.

You will need:
small glass
index card (large enough to fit over the mouth of the glass)
water

1. Fill the glass with water.
2. Place the index card over the mouth of the glass.
3. Holding the card FIRMLY with one hand, turn the glass upside down as shown. Let go of the index card.

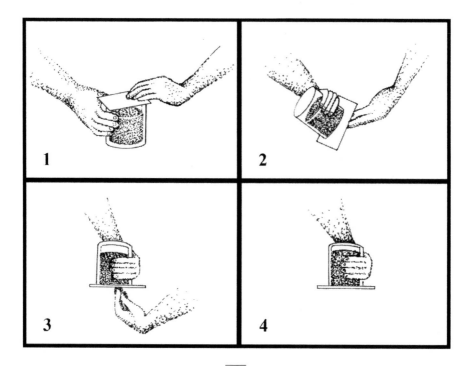

What happens?
Surprise! The index card stays in place, keeping the water in the glass.

Why?
Air pressure keeps the index card on the glass. Believe it or not, the force of the air pressure pushing upward is harder than the pressure of the water pushing downward. Amazing what something invisible can do!

You use air pressure when you drink through a straw. By taking a sip, you suck out some of the air inside the straw. This lowers the air pressure inside the straw. The greater pressure of the air *outside* the straw pushes on the surface of your drink. This helps push the liquid up through the straw and into your mouth.

Try This!

What do you think would happen if:

- you turned the glass sideways instead of upside down? Does the water spill out? (*Hint:* Air pushes equally in all directions.)
- you poked holes in the index card before you placed it over the glass and turned it upside down? Does the water leak out? (*Hint:* The answer has to do with the invisible skin created on water through surface tension. See Things Are Getting Tense, page 51.)
- you used a sheet of paper instead of an index card?
- you used a pin to poke one or two small holes in a straw, and then tried to drink through it?

Under Pressure

LEVEL: 1

This experiment starts out like Balloon Blast (page 16), but then it takes a different turn. Is it magic? Nah . . . air pressure!

You will need:
empty 1- or 2-liter soda bottle
balloon that fits over the mouth of the bottle
bowl of hot (not scalding) water

1. Stretch the mouth of the balloon over the mouth of the soda bottle.
2. Hold the bottle and balloon in the bowl of hot water and wait for it to heat up. The hot air will expand and cause the balloon to inflate.
3. Take out the bottle with the balloon still attached and place in the refrigerator for about five minutes.

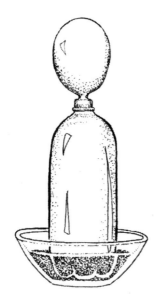
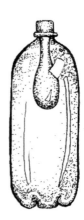

What happens?
The balloon is pushed into the bottle.

Why?
As air cools, air pressure decreases. The air pressure inside the balloon was lowered when it was placed in the refrigerator. The higher pressure of the air outside the balloon pushed on the balloon and forced it into the bottle.

Eggs-traordinary!

ADULT HELP REQUIRED   LEVEL: 2

This experiment is fun, but a little messy. Lay newspapers on the floor and over your work area to make cleanup easier.

You will need:
newspapers
hard-boiled egg
matches
empty glass bottle with narrow neck (but wide enough to put lit matches in)

1. Peel the shell off the egg.
2. Light three matches and drop them into the empty glass bottle.
3. Lay the egg over the opening of the bottle. Observe what happens to the lit matches, and then to the egg.

What happens?
Whoosh! The egg is sucked right into the bottle!

Why?
The lit matches heat the air inside the bottle, making it expand. As it expands, some of it escapes from the bottle. Eventually, the matches go out from lack of oxygen (because the egg is blocking the opening of the bottle). The air inside the bottle cools off and contracts, or takes up less space, and the air pressure decreases. Now the pressure inside the bottle is lower than it is outside. The greater pressure outside the bottle pushes the egg into the bottle.

HOW CAN AN AQUARIUM BE EMPTIED WITHOUT LIFTING IT?

Whenever you've visited your local pet store or aquarium supply shop, have you ever wondered just how they empty those big huge fish tanks? It's easier than you think.

Going with the Flow

LEVEL: 3

This is a variation of what you did in Water on the Move (page 63), but on a much larger (fish) scale. (Sorry—just couldn't resist!)

You will need:
2 pails or buckets
water
tabletop
flexible plastic or rubber tube, about 3 feet (91 cm) long (available at hardware stores)

1. Fill one pail with water and place it on the table. This will serve as your "aquarium."
2. Place the other pail on the floor next to the table.
3. Fill the tube completely with water. Cover both ends of the tube with your thumbs so no water can escape.
4. Quickly put one end of the tube in the pail full of water. Put the other end of the tube in the empty pail.
5. Take your thumbs off the ends of the tube.

What happens?
The water flows—*uphill, and then downhill*—from the full pail into the empty one through the tube.

Why?
Air pressure at your service. You made a *siphon*. When you took your thumb off the lower end of the tube, some of the water flowed out. This left a space behind it. Air pressure pushing on the surface of the water in the pail pushed water through the tube to fill that empty space. This continued until the pail was emptied into the other pail. Air pressure is strong enough to defy gravity.

What do you think would happen if you tried this experiment in outer space? Would it work?

DOES AIR PRESSURE HELP US BREATHE?

Look in a medical encyclopedia, an anatomy book, or on the Internet to find an illustration of the human respiratory system. Find the *diaphragm* (DY-uh-fram); it's a large muscle underneath your lungs that stretches across your entire body. When you take a breath, or *inhale*, your diaphragm moves down and your ribs move upward and outward. This increases the size of your body cavity and, at the same time, decreases the air pressure inside it. Thus, the pressure is lower inside your body cavity than outside your body. The greater air pressure outside your body pushes air through your nose or mouth and down into your lungs.

When you breathe out, or *exhale*, your diaphragm moves up and your ribs move downward and inward. This raises the pressure inside your body higher than outside, pushing the air out of your lungs.

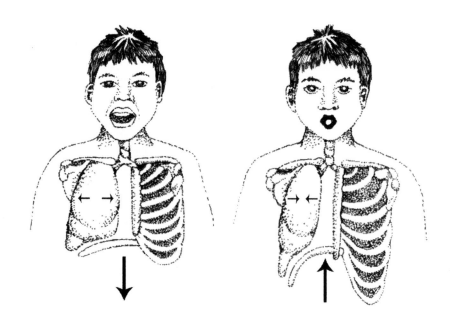

A Pressing Matter

ADULT HELP REQUIRED   LEVEL: 2

What happens when the forces of air pressure (inside and outside) are not equalized? Here's a simple, cool way to find out.

You will need:
funnel
empty 1- or 2-liter soda bottle with cap
extremely hot water

1. Place the funnel in the mouth of the soda bottle.
2. Pour the hot water into the funnel until the bottle is about one-quarter full. Immediately remove the funnel.
3. Screw the cap on quickly to prevent steam from escaping.

What happens?
The bottle crumples in on itself, pushed by a seemingly invisible force.

Why?
The hot water heats the air inside the bottle. The air expands and rises. Even though the cap is on, air is still forced out of the bottle. The air pressure inside the bottle therefore decreases. The greater pressure of the air outside the bottle pushes on the bottle and squashes it.

Try This!

Now unscrew and remove the bottle cap. What happens?

HOW DOES A FLY WALK ON THE CEILING?

It'd be impossible for you to walk on the ceiling—unless, of course, you're Spider-Man. So how does a fly do it? You also may be wondering what a question like this is doing in the Air section. Do these experiments and see for yourself.

Taking the Plunge

LEVEL: 1

Grab a friend to help you take the plunge on this one.

You will need:
2 plungers
water
a volunteer

1. First, wet the insides of the suction cups of both plungers.
2. You and your friend each take a plunger. Match the rims of the suction cups together.
3. Working together, push on both plungers until the air has been squeezed out from inside the suction cups.
4. Now try to pull them apart.

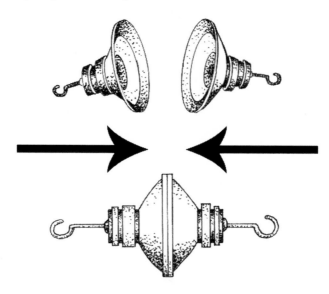

What happens?
The plungers appear to be stuck together. You will have a great deal of trouble trying to pull them apart.

Why?
When you and your buddy pushed the plungers together, you squeezed out most of the air that was trapped inside. By doing so, you lowered the air pressure inside the cups. This air pressure on the outside was strong enough to keep the cups together. The water you used to wet the plunger forms a seal (surface tension) and keeps air from getting back in.

So, how *does* a fly walk on the ceiling?

A fly's feet are shaped like suction cups. When the fly pushes its feet against a flat surface, most of the air is squeezed out. This leaves the pressure of the outside air strong enough to hold the fly to whatever surface it's on. When a fly moves, it picks up three of its six feet at a time. That's how it can move and stay on the ceiling at the same time. Do you think it would make a difference if the fly's feet are wet?

Try This!

If you have only one plunger, you can do a variation of this experiment. Wet the inside of the cup. Find a smooth, hard surface, such as the outside wall of your house or the wall around your backyard. Put the suction cup flat on the surface and push hard. Now try to pull the plunger off.

Here's another one you can do with some small plastic or rubber suction cups (available at hardware stores). Try lifting objects that have different surfaces. Do the suction cups stick best against rough surfaces? Smooth? Bumpy? Soft? Why? Wet the suction cups. Do they stick any better? Why?

That's News to Me

ADULT SUPERVISION SUGGESTED   LEVEL: 2

This is a great experiment that will amaze your friends again and again. Just make sure you have a lot of rulers handy . . .

You will need:
plastic or wooden ruler (one that you don't need anymore)
table
2 sheets of newspaper (large size, not tabloid size)

1. Place the ruler on the table, allowing 3 inches (8 cm) to hang over the edge of the table.
2. Open the two sheets of newspaper and smooth them out. Lay them over the ruler, leaving the 3 inches uncovered.
3. Hit the end of the ruler hard.

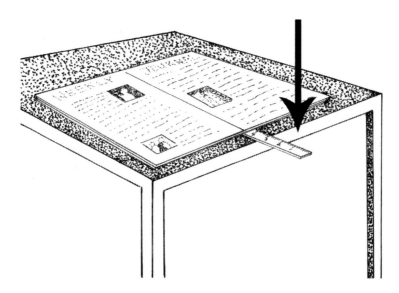

What happens?
Amazingly, the newspaper does not move. Even more amazingly, the ruler might break in half.

Why?

When you consider what you've learned about air pressure, the result of this experiment is not surprising. We know that the blanket of air that surrounds the planet Earth presses down with a great deal of force. (A weight of almost 15 pounds is pressed on every square inch of surface.) This air pressure is strong enough even to keep a flimsy sheet of newspaper in place. Now it's off to the store to buy more rulers...

WHAT GIVES AN AIRPLANE LIFT?

An average airplane weighs about 27 tons (that's 54,000 pounds!), and that's *without* all the passengers, luggage, and fuel. Even with its powerful engines, how can something so huge and heavy climb into the air and stay there?

Blown Away

LEVEL: 2

In this experiment, a sheet of paper provides the basic design that helps an airplane fly: a simple curve.

You will need:
sheet of paper
scissors
ruler
tape
table or desk

1. Cut the paper so that it measures 3 x 8 inches (8 x 20 cm).
2. Fold the paper so that one side is a little longer than the other. Unfold.
3. Line up the two short edges of the paper and tape them together. The longer side of the paper should curve outward, and the short side should be flat.
4. Tape the paper to the edge of the table, curved side up.
5. Blow gently across the curved top of the paper. What do you see? Blow harder.

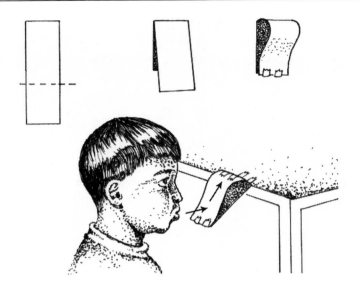

What happens?
You'd think that the paper would blow down, since you're blowing across the top of it. Instead, it is lifted into the air.

Why?
Your paper is flat underneath and curved on top, like the wing of an airplane. The curve on the top gives the paper its lifting power. The shape of the paper creates greater air pressure on the bottom, pushing the paper up.

So, what *does* give an airplane lift?

As an airplane moves, its wings split the air. Air goes over and under the wing. Because the top of the wing is curved, the distance across the top is longer than the distance under the wing. Yet the streams of air that move across the top and across the bottom of the wing meet at nearly the same time on the other side. Because the air going over the wing curves and travels farther, it must speed up to arrive at the rear of the wing at almost the same instant as the air that is going under. This faster-moving air creates lower air pressure. The slower-moving air under the wing has a greater air pressure. It pushes up harder than the air above the wing pushes down, causing the wing to rise. Thus the airplane is lifted through the air.

This phenomenon is called the *Bernoulli* (ber-NOO-lee) *principle*. In the 1700s, a mathematician named Daniel Bernoulli found that the faster a stream of fluid (that is, a liquid or a gas) is flowing, the less it pushes outward from the side of the stream, and the more it decreases in pressure.

Try This!

Cut another strip of paper 10 x 2 inches (25 x 5 cm). Hold the short end of the paper just under your mouth. Blow across the top of the paper. It rises. As the airstream rushes across the top of the paper, the air pressure decreases. Underneath the paper, the pressure is greater, pushing the paper up.

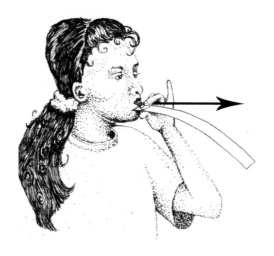

Lying Low

LEVEL: 1

Cut a 4 x 4-inch (10 x 10 cm) piece out of a plastic ziploc bag. On a table, place two books of equal size about 1 1/2 inches apart. Lay the piece of plastic across the space between the books. Try to blow the plastic off. Not so easy to do, is it?

Blowing It

LEVEL: 2

Here's another example of how air pressure works. Think you know what will happen? Think again!

You will need:
string
scissors
ruler
tape
2 Ping-Pong balls or small balloons, inflated
short straw

1. Cut two lengths of string, each 24 inches long.
2. Tape one Ping-Pong ball to each string.
3. Hang the two strings and balls about 4 inches (10 cm) apart on the back of a chair or the edge of a table (use tape to fasten the ends of the string to the chair or table)
4. Predict what will happen when you blow between the Ping-Pong balls. Now blow. Were you right?

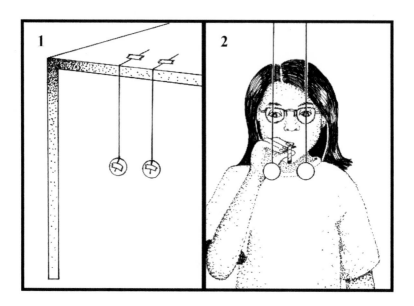

What happens?
Instead of blowing away from each other, the Ping-Pong balls are pushed together.

Why?
It's the Bernoulli principle once again. The pressure of the faster-moving air between the two balls is lower than the pressure of the surrounding air. Can you figure out the rest?

A Funnel Thing Happened...

LEVEL: 1

Place a Ping-Pong ball inside a funnel. Hold the ball inside with your finger and turn the funnel upside down. Blow hard through the funnel. As you blow, let go of the ball. Does the ball come out?

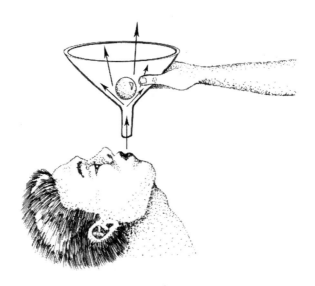

In a Vacuum

LEVEL: 3

Can you figure out how to use a vacuum cleaner to make a Ping-Pong ball float? First, connect the hose of a vacuum cleaner to the "wrong" end. Turn on the vacuum cleaner so that air is blowing out. Place the ball in the airstream. (This can also be done with a hair dryer, but only with one that has a cold setting. Otherwise the Ping-Pong ball will melt.)

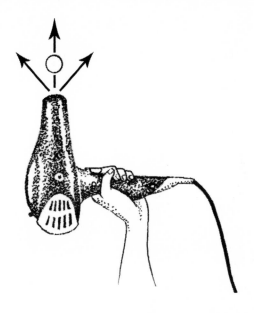

HOW DOES A SUBMARINE WORK?

When you're swimming and you dive down into the water, you can't stay down very long because you naturally float back up to the surface (not to mention you can't hold your breath forever!). That's partly because the air in your body keeps you from sinking. How does a submarine submerge if it's got air inside too?

Squeeze Play

LEVEL: 2

To find out how a submarine submerges, you'll be making your very own mini-sub.

You will need:
empty 2-liter plastic soda bottle with cap
water
medicine dropper

1. Fill the soda bottle to the top with water.
2. Fill the medicine dropper with about a half inch (1.3 cm) of water.
3. Place the dropper in the bottle. It should float near the top. (You may need to adjust the amount of water inside the dropper.)
4. Screw the cap on.
5. Squeeze the sides of the bottle gently with both hands. Observe the dropper. Now let go of the bottle.

What happens?
When the bottle is squeezed, the dropper sinks to the bottom. When the sides are released, the dropper rises back to the top.

Why?
Squeezing the bottle pushes the air in the dropper into a smaller space. Water from the bottle fills this space. This makes the dropper heavier, and it sinks. When you let go of the bottle, the air in the dropper returns to its original volume, pushing the water out. The dropper becomes lighter and floats back up. Air can be *compressed*, or squeezed into a smaller space. Water cannot be compressed, so when it is under pressure it moves into whatever space is available.

So, how *does* a submarine work?

Submarines have ballast tanks that can be filled with water and emptied of water. When a submarine is on the surface of the ocean, air pressure is used to keep water out of the ballast tanks so that the submarine stays afloat. To submerge, the tanks are filled with water so they become heavier. When the submarine resurfaces, air pressure blows the water out of the tanks, making the submarine lighter.

What Do You Think?

Compressed air can be used to lift an automobile. How is this possible? Do research on your own to find out how.

Whatever Floats Your Boat

LEVEL: 1

It's your density—er, your *destiny*—to learn a new scientific principle by doing this experiment.

You will need:
empty glass bottle, any size, with cap
container large enough to hold the bottle
water

1. Fill the container with water. (You can make a container by asking a grown-up to cut the top off a large plastic water or milk container.) Predict what will happen when you put the bottle in.
2. Screw the cap onto the bottle and put it in the container. Were you correct?
3. Now take the cap off the bottle and let it fill with water. What does it do?

What happens?
When you put the bottle in the water, it floats, even though you may have predicted it would sink because it's glass. When you take the cap off, the bottle fills with water and sinks.

Why?
The bottle floats because the glass and the air inside are not as *dense* as the water. In general, *density* is a measure of how much material is in a certain space. It is often used to determine how much something weighs. Even though the glass is solid, it is not as dense as water because water takes up more space. When you took the cap off, the water came in and filled the air space. Together, the glass and water became more dense than the surrounding water, and the bottle sank.

Try This!

Can you make just the right combination of air and water in the glass bottle so that it floats *between* the top and the bottom of the water in the container?

Did You Know?

When an object floats on top of water (like the glass bottle with air), it has *positive buoyancy* (BOY-un-see). When an object sinks in water (like the glass bottle filled with water), it has *negative buoyancy*. When it floats between the top and bottom (like the bottle with both air and water), it has *neutral buoyancy*.

This Must Be Displace

LEVEL: 3

To understand how a boat floats, you need to understand how *displacement* works.

You will need:
string
scissors
assorted objects that will sink (rocks, coins, screws, keys, etc.)
pie tin
plastic medicine dosage cup
2 plastic cups, one with a spout (you can make this yourself—see the illustration)
water
pencil and paper
paper towels for cleanup

1. Cut lengths of string 12 inches long and tie one to each of the assorted objects. (If you can't tie it, tape it on.)
2. Set the pie tin on a tabletop. Place the medicine dosage cup in the tin. Put the spouted plastic cup next to the pie tin. This will serve as the overflow cup. The spout should be aimed at the medicine cup. (See illustration.)
3. Fill the spouted cup with water until it just starts to overflow.
4. Holding an object by the attached string, carefully lower it into the overflow cup. Record the amount of water that spills into the medicine cup. Tip the water out.
5. Repeat steps 3 and 4 with each remaining object.

What happens?
A different amount of water spills out depending on the object that is placed in the overflow cup. If you weighed the amount of water spilled out by each object, it would weigh the same as the object.

Why?
Each object *displaced* the water in the overflow cup. If you fill your bathtub to the very top and then get into it, it spills out over the side. Your body pushes some of the water out and fills up the space left behind. You have displaced the water.

If you put a toy boat in the bathtub, the boat would take up space and displace some of the water. Collect the water that was displaced, and it would weigh the same as the boat does.

WHY CAN YOU LIFT YOUR BIG BROTHER IN A SWIMMING POOL?

It's mind-boggling: When you and your brother are in the water, you can lift him with ease. But out of the water, it's not so easy. How is that possible?

Take a Load Off

LEVEL: 3

Can a rock lose weight? It can, and without even dieting!

You will need:
string
rock
spring scale
paper and pencil
deep container of water

1. Tie a string around the rock.
2. Weigh the rock using the spring scale. Record this weight.
3. Keeping the rock on the scale, carefully lower both into the container of water. (*Note:* Do not let the scale or rock touch the bottom of the container.) Record this weight.

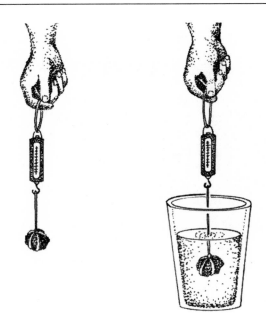

What happens?
The rock weighs *less* in the water than it did dry. Did it actually lose weight in the water?

Why?
Yes, the rock *seems* to weigh less in the water. It's based on the *Archimedes principle*. Archimedes (ar-kih-ME-deez) was a Greek mathematician and inventor who discovered that an object immersed in water is buoyed up, or pushed up, by a force that is equal to the weight of the water that is displaced. That's why your big brother appears to weigh less in water, and why huge ships and boats can float on water.

WHAT MAKES A BOAT FLOAT?

It's amazing that a boat—from a tiny rowboat to an enormous cruise ship—can float on water.

Foiled Again

ADULT HELP REQUIRED   LEVEL: 2

How much would it take for a boat to sink? Don't be dense—just do the following to find the answer.

You will need:
empty 1-gallon plastic milk or water jug
water
aluminum foil
scissors
stack of pennies
paper and pencil
felt-tip marker
paper towels for cleanup

1. Have a grownup cut off the top of the milk jug. This will be your displacement container. Fill it with water.
2. Cut a 5-inch (13 cm) square of aluminum foil.
3. Shape the foil square into a boat as shown. Place your boat in your displacement container.
4. Add the pennies to the boat one at a time. Determine how many pennies you can add before the boat sinks. Write this number down. Remove the pennies.
5. Use the marker to mark the water level on the side of the container.
6. Add the pennies to the boat again, one by one, until you reach the maximum number. Mark the new water level on the container.

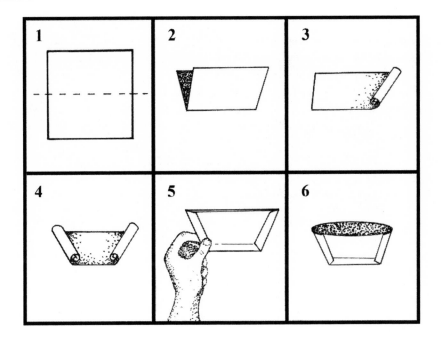

What happens?
The boat eventually sinks, as the water level of the container rises.

Why?
As pennies are added, the boat becomes denser than the water. It starts to take up more space, *displacing* the water. The water has nowhere else to go, so it rises higher. Eventually, the boat and pennies take up more space than the water, and the boat sinks (see Whatever Floats Your Boat, page 90).

Do objects sink because they are heavy, and float because they are light? Not really. A fork that weighs just a few ounces will sink, but an aircraft carrier weighing thousands of tons will float.

So, what *does* make a boat float?

It has to do with displacement, density, and buoyancy. In This Must Be Displace (page 92), you learned about *displacement*. Each sinking object displaced a certain amount of water.

Even though the cruise ship weighs several thousand tons, it is built large and wide enough to displace enough water that it floats instead of sinking. The ocean water is displaced, but because the ocean is so big, it does not overflow. Instead, the displaced water pushes back on the ship, giving it buoyancy and keeping it afloat (see Take a Load Off, page 94).

So, if a boat weighs 2,000 pounds, it pushes down on the water until 2,000 pounds of water have been displaced. That same amount of water pushes upward on the boat to make it float.

A rock is denser than a feather. Water is denser than air. Density has to do with how closely packed something is. Let's use sand as an example. If you scoop sand loosely into a container, that sand will have a loose density. If you shake the container gently and tap it several times, the sand will settle and get packed down. It takes up less space. This increases the density of the sand. Similarly, more people live in the city than in the countryside. The city is *more densely populated* than the countryside. Thus, if a boat is less dense than the water it displaces, it will float. If it is denser, it will sink.

Try This!

Flatten your aluminum-foil boat and drop it into the water. Does it still float? Now roll a piece of modeling clay into a ball. Drop it into the water. What happens? It sinks. Now mold the clay into a shape that will make it float. (Remember: density, buoyancy, displacement.)

What Do You Think?

Would a ship made of steel still float? After all, steel is much denser than water. But remember, a ship still has a lot of space on it that is *not* made of steel. This space is filled with air, and air is less dense than water. If you add all the steel and all the air inside together, it is not as dense as the water around it. Of course, if the ship ran into an iceberg and was torn open (like the *Titanic*), water would rush in and replace the air. This would make the entire ship more dense than the water, and it would sink.

LET THERE BE
LIGHT . . . AND COLOR

We need light to survive . . . literally. Without it, there would be little life on earth as we know it. Plants need light to grow, and animals and humans need to eat the plants, or eat the animals that eat the plants, in order to survive.

Light is energy that travels from the sun to the earth at a very fast speed. It takes a beam of light only 8 minutes to travel the 94.5 million miles (146 million km) from the sun to the earth. The speed of light is 186,000 miles (300,000 km) per second. Light takes only 1.3 seconds to go from the Earth to the moon, but it would take you nine years to walk the same distance. The distance that light travels in one year is called a light year.

Light travels in a straight line, but it can be bent, or *refracted*. As light passes from or through one medium to another, its speed changes, causing it to bend. Some materials refract light more than others do.

We create our own light through natural means, such as fire, and through artificial means, such as electricity, but our primary source of light is, of course, the sun. Light and heat are closely related. After all, the sun is able to give off so much light because it is so hot. Put your hand up to a lightbulb and you can feel the heat. Fire provides both light and heat.

Laser beams are made of light, but it is different from ordinary light. Laser light is of only one color and is high intensity. Because it spreads very little over long distances, it can be harnessed and controlled. Lasers can be aimed at a target to measure distances precisely, even distances in space. They are used in surgical tools, to scan bar codes, to transmit information, to "read" compact discs, and to produce fantastic light shows.

In this section, you'll learn how light creates mirror images, how light helps us to see, and what makes the colors in a rainbow. Is white light really white? Is black really black? How can you break a pencil in half without using your hands? You'll find out the answers to these and more.

WHY DO LEFT AND RIGHT LOOK REVERSED IN A MIRROR IMAGE?

We take for granted how much we rely on mirrors in our everyday lives. And if you've ever been in a funhouse, you know how much fun mirrors can be. But even ordinary mirrors can be fun, too.

Left, Right? No, Right, Left?

LEVEL: 1

Mirror, mirror, on the wall, is that my right ear after all . . . ?

You will need:
large mirror
rubber ball

1. Look at yourself in the mirror.
2. Touch your left ear with your left hand. Which ear are you touching in your reflection?
3. Bounce the rubber ball straight down toward the floor. What happens? Now bounce it at an angle. What's different?

What happens?
You appear to be touching your *right* ear, not your left. When you bounce the ball straight down, it bounces straight up. When bounced at an angle, it comes back at the same angle. This causes images we see in mirrors to be reversed.

Why?
An image is what you see in a mirror. The image in the mirror is reversed. The image seems to face you. If you raise your right hand, your image will raise its left hand, and if you wink your left eye, the image will wink its right eye.

The image in the mirror is the same size as the object in front of it. And the image in the mirror seems to be just as far behind the mirror as the object in front of it.

Lighten Up

LEVEL: 3

In this experiment, you'll discover where light travels after it is reflected off a mirror.

You will need:
plain white paper and black construction paper
pencil and ruler or straight edge
ruler
tape
small mirror
small box or wooden block
scissors
flashlight

1. On the plain white paper, make a chart and label it like the one shown here. There should be 2 cm. between each position.
2. Tape the mirror so that it is standing straight up on the small box. Place the box and mirror on the spot as shown.
3. Cut a circle out of the black construction paper. It should be large enough to cover the front (bulb) of the flashlight.
4. Cut a small slit in the paper circle. Tape the circle to the flashlight. Turn the flashlight on.
5. Hold the flashlight at position L3 (Left 3) and aim the beam at the center mark where the mirror is. Where does the light fall?
6. Repeat step 5 for position L2, then L1, noting the light's position for each. Do the same for R3, R2, and R1.

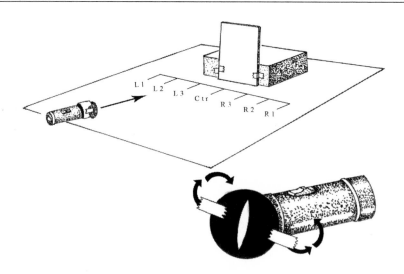

What happens?
When the flashlight is held at position L1, the light beam finishes at R1.
When it is held at L2, the light finishes at R2.

Why?
The reason for this is called the "Law of Reflection." This means that
when a light ray strikes a mirror straight down, up, or forward, the ray is
reflected directly back.

When a ray of light strikes a mirror at a slant, or angle, the ray is
reflected at a slant, or angle, in the opposite direction.

Letter Perfect

LEVEL: 2

On a sheet of paper, print the alphabet in large capital letters. Some of the letters of the alphabet are *symmetrical,* meaning that if you drew a line through the middle either horizontally or vertically, the two halves are equal reflections of each other. Letters that are equal on top and bottom have *horizontal symmetry.* Letters that are equal from left to right have *vertical symmetry.*

Which letters do you think will have horizontal symmetry? Which will have vertical symmetry? Which will have both? Now place a small mirror down the middle of each letter, first horizontally, then vertically. How many letters did you guess right?

B, C, D, E, K have horizontal symmetry.

A, M, T, U, V, W, Y have vertical symmetry.

H, I, O, X have both.

Word Play

LEVEL: 2

Print these words in capital letters on a sheet of paper.

PUP	DICE	TUBA	BOX
DID	HIKE	NOON	HEX

Hold the paper in front of a mirror. Which words can you still read?

Try This!

Create a secret message to a friend by writing the words in a way that they can be read only by looking at them in a mirror. Give the message to your friend and see if he or she can figure out how to decode it.

WHY DOES AN OBJECT LOOK BROKEN OR IN A DIFFERENT PLACE WHEN IT'S IN WATER?

A bear can easily pull fish out of a stream or river. However, if you drop a penny into water and reach in to pick it up, it does not seem to be in the same place as your hand is. And if you look at your hand from the side, it looks like it's broken. What do bears know that we don't?

Give Me a Break

LEVEL: 1

Learn how to "break" a pencil in half *without* using your hands.

You will need:
clear drinking glass
water
pencil

1. Fill the glass halfway with water.
2. Place the pencil in the glass.
3. Look at the pencil through the side of the glass.

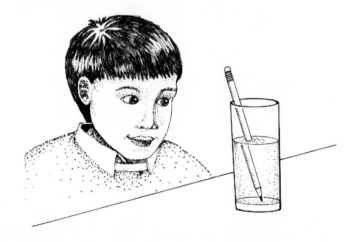

What happens?
The pencil appears to be broken.

Why?

The light that is reflected off the part of the pencil below the water bends when it hits the surface. When you see the part of the pencil that is not in the water, you are looking at it from a different direction. This is called *refraction*. That's why the pencil appears to be broken. Bears instinctively know that an object in water is not always where it appears to be, so they make adjustments when they're hunting fish.

Light acts as a wave. The speed of this wave in air and in space is about 186,00 miles per second—the speed of light. This is fast enough to go around the earth in the time it takes you to blink. Light takes 8 minutes to reach the earth from the sun. But light slows down as it travels into materials such as glass and water.

Try This!

What do you think would happen if you put the pencil in a glass of corn syrup? How about a glass of rubbing alcohol? Would it still appear bent? Which liquid would bend the pencil the most? Which liquid would bend it the least? (*Note:* The denser the liquid, the more the pencil will appear to bend.)

HOW DO OUR EYES WORK?

The eye works just like a miniature camera. It has a lens, and at the back of the eye is the *retina* (RET-in-uh), which acts like film or a computer chip to record the images you see.

Seeing the Light

LEVEL: 1

Here's how to make a penny "disappear" and reappear. It's a great trick to show your friends. Master it on your own first, then have your friends step up while you pour the water. To figure out how this experiment works, apply what you just learned about refraction (see Give Me a Break, page 105).

You will need:
glass measuring cup
water
small, clean empty tuna can
penny

1. Fill the measuring cup with water.
2. Place the can on a table or the kitchen countertop. Put the penny in the can.
3. Bend down until the top edge of the can blocks your view of the penny.
4. Without moving or changing your line of sight, pick up the measuring cup and *slowly* pour water into the can.

What happens?
As you pour water into the can, the penny seems to "float" into view.

Why?
In order to see something, light must reach your eyes. If light—whether it's sunlight, artificial light, or another source—is not reflected, or bounced off, from the object to your eyes, and if the object itself does not give off its own light, you cannot see it. The light reflected off the penny is stopped from reaching your eyes by the tuna can, which is *opaque*, meaning that it blocks light. You can't see through it, and thus you can't see the penny.

When water is added, however, the light reflected off the penny passes through the water. When it gets to the surface of the water, it bends, or *refracts*, around the edge of the can and reaches your eyes. The penny "floats" into view. When light enters a material that you can see through, such as glass or water, the light rays slow down and bend.

Objects do not always seem to be *what* they are or *where* they are. It's not magic . . . it's science!

Did You Know?

Have you ever wondered how cats and other nocturnal animals can see in the dark? Actually, if it's completely dark (in other words, no light at all), cats can't see anything. But if there is a tiny bit of light (and even at nighttime there is some light), cats can see. The pupils of their eyes *dilate* (DY-late), or get bigger. This lets in more light, allowing the cat to see. Owls have very large pupils, helping them to hunt at night.

But our pupils dilate too, so why can't we see as well as cats do? Cats and other animals have a *crystalline* (KRIS-tull-in) layer in their eyes that we don't have. When light gets in, this layer reflects it all around the eye, allowing the animal to see better. This is also what causes an animal's eyes to shine in the dark.

The Secret's Out

LEVEL: 3

Break out the spy gear! You're on your way to becoming a real Spy Kid when you make this cool secret decoder.

You will need:
paper and pencil or pen
mirror
long, empty glass cylindrical jar (label removed) with lid (such as an olive jar)
water

1. Think of a secret message. Put it on paper, writing the letters upside down and in reverse. Use a mirror to help you.
2. Fill the jar to the top with water. Screw the lid on tight.
3. Turn the jar on its side. Hold it above the message you wrote.
4. Look through the liquid in the jar at your message. Focus by moving the jar closer and farther away from you.

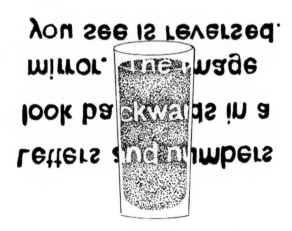

What happens?
Once you adjust the focus, you can clearly read and understand the secret message you wrote.

Why?

The jar and the water act like a lens. The lens focuses the light that is reflected off the paper and creates an image of what is on the paper. This image is upside down and reversed. Because that is how you wrote the message, your makeshift lens turned the letters the right way, and you are able to read the message.

Did You Know?

A lens is a transparent object that has at least one curved surface. There are two basic types of lenses. A *convex* lens is thicker in the middle than at the edges. An image seen through this type of lens is usually bigger than the object being viewed, and it is also inverted (upside down). A *concave* lens is thicker at the edges than in the middle. It bends light so that the light spreads out. The image seen is usually smaller than the object and not inverted.

Lenses are used in all kinds of everyday equipment: eyeglasses, microscopes, telescopes, binoculars, cameras, film projectors, and, of course, your very own eyes. Your eyes have convex lenses that collect light from an object and focus a small image of the object onto your retina at the back of your eye. It's similar to how a camera works. When you look at an object, the lens in your eye projects a picture of that object onto your retina. The image is upside down. Your brain turns the picture the right way and tells you what you're looking at. This happens so fast you are not even aware of it.

IS BLACK INK REALLY BLACK?

Well, it certainly looks black, and the label says black. But is it really? The answer may surprise you. Remember, in science, things are not always what they seem.

Getting Down to Basics

LEVEL: 3

You will need:
scissors
white coffee filter paper
ruler
water-soluble black marker
tape
pencil
drinking glass
water

1. Cut a strip from the coffee filter paper, 10 x 1 inches (25 x 3 cm).
2. Use the marker and press down hard to make a heavy black dot about 2 inches (5 cm) from one end of the strip. Let the spot dry. (If you are in a hurry, use a hair dryer.)
3. Tape the paper strip to the middle of the pencil.
4. Fill the glass with water about 3/4 of an inch deep.
5. Holding the pencil, dip the end of the paper strip into the water. Make sure the strip does not touch the sides of the glass, and make sure the black dot does not get wet.
6. Watch what happens to the strip as it soaks up the water. When the water has almost reached the top of the strip, take it out and let it dry. Now look at the strip.

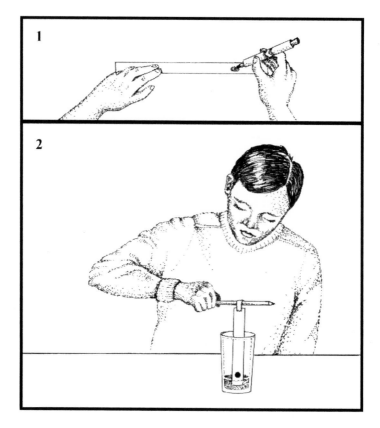

What happens?

The "black" marker dot seems to have disappeared. In its place are many different colors, each in a different place.

Why?

What you are looking at are all the colors that are combined to make the color black. Like most colors, black is actually a mixture of several different pigments, or colors. The filter paper you used is *porous* (PORE-us), or full of tiny openings that allow in water. When the filter is dipped in water, the water, along with any dyes it contains, moves up through the paper. A different band of color is formed for each dye, because each one moves up the paper in a different way, forming a pattern called a *chromatogram* (kroh-MA-toh-gram). That's why each color appeared at a different spot. Use this experiment to determine the different colors used in any color of marker.

Try This!

Repeat this experiment using Kool-Aid instead of a black marker. Use the tip of a toothpick to place a drop of Kool-Aid on the paper strip. Is Kool-Aid made up of different colors too?

Next, gather two or more different brands of water-soluble black markers and do the experiment again. Is each brand made up of the same colors? Do they make exactly the same chromatograms?

HOW CAN A PENNY BE USED TO MAKE MORE PENNIES?

You've heard about making your money grow, but *literally?*

Magic Mirrors

LEVEL: 3

You will need:
masking tape
2 mirrors, 2 x 2 3/4 inches (5 x 7 cm), or 2 small mirrors of equal size
paper and pencil
ruler
penny

1. Tape the two mirrors, shiny sides together, so they open like a book.
2. With the paper, pencil, and ruler, make a worksheet like the one shown here.
3. Open up your mirror "book" all the way and place it on the solid horizontal line. Line it up with the center mark.
4. Place the penny flat on the circle.
5. Bend the mirrors so that they line up on the dotted lines marked A. Look in the mirrors and record the number of pennies you see, including the one on the worksheet.
6. Bend the mirrors again to line up on the lines marked B. Record the number of pennies. Repeat for lines C and D.

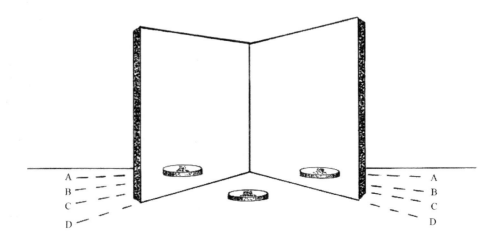

What happens?
When the mirrors are wide open, you see three coins: one in each mirror and one on the worksheet. As the mirrors are brought closer together—in other words, as the angle is narrowed—you see more images of the coin. You have "made" more money.

WHY?
Light rays bounce off the coin and hit the mirror. These light rays are reflected back and forth between the two mirrors before they reach your eyes. The reflected light lets you see more than one coin. The closer the mirrors, the more the light bounces back and forth, and the more images you see.

Try This!

Center a sharp pencil between the two mirrors, with the pencil point touching the place where the two mirrors join. Predict what you will see when you look in the mirrors. How might you get more images of the pencil? How might you get fewer images?

What Do You Think?

Which would get more reflections, a smaller angle or a larger angle? If you were designing a revolving door made of mirrors, how many sections would you create? (Remember, a person still has to fit in the door.)

Did You Know?

A mirror is a flat piece of glass that has been polished smooth. The back of the glass is covered with a thin coating of silver or other shiny metal. When light strikes the mirror, it passes through the transparent glass and is reflected off the shiny backing. The reflected light sends back an image—a reflection—of whatever is in front of the mirror. As you learned in the experiments earlier in this section, the image in a mirror is reversed because of the way the light is reflected. However, an image in a flat mirror is exactly the same size as the object in front of it.

WHERE DO THE COLORS IN A RAINBOW COME FROM?

Nothing brings a smile more than seeing a beautiful rainbow. From a simple bead to a garden hose to the rain that falls from the sky, there are numerous ways to create this amazing natural phenomenon.

Color Me Curious

LEVEL: 1

The colors you see are not always what they seem. Do this experiment and find out why.

You will need:
diffraction grating (available from a science supply store)
lamp with a clear bulb

1. Turn on the lamp. Hold the diffraction grating in front of the lamp bulb. Predict what color or colors you will see when you look through it.
2. Look through the diffraction grating at the bulb.

What happens?
Did you think you would see only white, because the light is white? Instead, what you see are the seven colors that make up a rainbow: red, orange, yellow, green, blue, indigo, and violet. (Notice there is no white.) These colors are called the *spectrum* and make up the light that we see. The seven colors are always the same, and they are always in the same order.

Why?
The diffraction grating split the light from the bulb into the spectrum of colors that make up the light. Raindrops also work like a diffraction grating, creating the rainbows that you often see in the sky.

Try This!

Try creating a rainbow with bubbles, a thin layer of cooking oil, the spray from a garden hose, a prism, or a piece of cut glass or crystal, such as a bead or figurine or candy dish. Use sunlight or a flashlight as your light source. If you hold the shiny side of a CD, DVD, or CD-ROM under a bright light, you will see the spectrum of colors displayed across the surface of the disc.

A Different Angle

LEVEL: 2

Fill a glass baking dish halfway with water. Angle a small mirror in the water in one corner of the dish. Use a piece of clay to hold the mirror in place (see illustration). Shine a flashlight through the water and onto the mirror. You should see a rainbow on the wall or ceiling. (If this doesn't work, adjust the mirror or move the dish.)

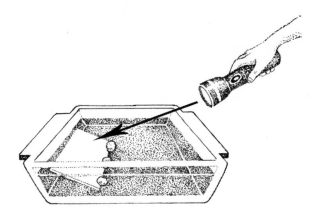

SOUNDING OFF

We live in a world filled with all types of sounds. Babies cry, dogs bark, engines roar, bells ring, people chatter. In fact, if the entire world suddenly fell into total silence, we would not know what to do. Sound reassures us of all the vibrant life that surrounds us.

Sounds that may be beautiful and soothing to one person may sound unpleasant to another. Simply put, sound is what you perceive when vibrations enter your ears. But what exactly creates sound? When a door slams, or when you clap your hands, how does that movement make a sound? What makes us hear? How can something as basic as air make beautiful music?

Like heat and light, sound is a form of energy. It is produced by motion. When an object moves, it causes the matter surrounding it—solid, liquid, or gas—to vibrate. The vibration creates sound. When air vibrates, it creates little waves, called *sound waves*, that travel through the air from its source to our ears.

Sounds can be absorbed or reflected. If you've been in a crowded restaurant that has hardwood floors, bare walls, and wooden chairs, you've no doubt noticed how loud and noisy it is. But carpet the floor, cover the walls with artwork, and put padding on the wooden chairs, and things are noticeably quieter. Hard surfaces reflect sound, soft surfaces absorb them.

Sound waves can bounce back and forth against hard surfaces, much like light rays are reflected off a mirror. An *echo* is the same sound heard at least twice. Walk into a tunnel and call out "Hello!" You will hear "Hello!" a second time . . . or perhaps more. Some animals use echoes to determine where they are or to locate prey. Both bats and whales emit sounds as they move about. If the sound bounces back quickly, the animal knows something is close. If it takes longer, the animal knows the object is far away.

In this section, you'll use a variety of ordinary household items—from rubber bands to drinking straws to table salt—to learn about how sound works. You'll also learn about the properties of sound such as volume and pitch. Sounds good, doesn't it? Then let's get started!

WHAT IS SOUND?

Just how is sound created, and how does it move through the air? How do our ears work, and what exactly are they hearing? These next few experiments will help you find the answers.

Good Vibrations

LEVEL: 1

You're about to learn just how those odd-looking organs on either side of your head work. Contrary to popular belief, things don't necessarily go in one ear and out the other...

You will need:
rubber band
a friend

1. Hold the rubber band. Grab the other end with your free hand.
2. Spread your arms wide to stretch out the rubber band. Have your friend pluck the rubber band in the middle. (You can also do this experiment by yourself. Just loop one end of the rubber band around something stationary, such as a bedpost. Then you can pluck the rubber band with your free hand.) Observe what you hear and what the rubber band does.

What happens?
The rubber band moves rapidly back and forth, up and down, or *vibrates.* You hear it make a *ping* sound.

Why?
The rubber band's vibrations also cause the air around the rubber band to vibrate, producing sound waves. These sound waves travel to your ears and make your eardrums vibrate. (The shape of your ears help catch the sound waves.) In turn, these vibrations move to your inner ear, where they are picked up by three tiny bones. These bones tap on a fluid-filled area inside your ear and change into electrical signals. Nerves then carry these signals to your brain, and your brain tells you what you are hearing: the *ping* sound.

Getting in Tune

LEVEL: 1

See if you can get a tuning fork (available where musical instruments are sold). Strike the tuning fork against something hard, like a table. Hold it to your ear. What do you hear? How does the tuning fork feel in your hand? Strike the tuning fork again and dip it into an ice cube tray filled with water. Surprise! You have a shower. And, just for fun, strike the tuning fork and touch the end of it to your teeth. Makes you tingly all over, doesn't it?

Speak Up!

LEVEL: 1

Place one or two fingers lightly on the middle of your throat. Say something . . . anything. Tell a joke or sing. Do you feel your vocal cords vibrating? When you talk, you make air come out of your lungs. The air passes over your vocal cords and makes them vibrate. The vibration causes the surrounding air to move (like the rubber band in Good Vibrations, page 120), and the sound emerges from your mouth.

Did You Know?

A bee moves its wings back and forth more than two hundred times a second. Can you figure out how bees buzz?

WHAT IS VOLUME?

From a whisper to a rock concert to a jet engine, we all know that volume has to do with how loud something gets. But just how is volume created? Aside from turning a knob, that is.

Loud and Clear

LEVEL:1

If anyone else is around, give a warning that things are about to get LOUD with this experiment. Tell them it's all in the name of science!

You will need:
tablespoon
salt
aluminum pie tin
source of music with exterior speakers (such as a portable stereo or radio), large enough for the pie tin to sit on top

1. Add 1 tablespoon of salt to the pie tin. Place the pie tin on top of the portable stereo.
2. Turn the music on at a fairly low volume. Observe the salt. Turn the music up louder, then louder and louder, watching the salt each time you boost the volume.

What happens?
As the music gets louder, the grains of salt jump faster and higher.

Why?
Sounds can be loud or soft. This is the *volume* of the sound. Volume is the amount of energy a sound wave carries. The greater the source of energy, the stronger the vibration, and the louder the sound. The stronger the vibration, the more the salt moves.

Did You Know?

Volume is measured in *decibels*. The rustling of leaves is less than 20 decibels. If you are talking in a normal voice, you are talking at about 50 decibels. A vacuum cleaner is about 80 decibels. A jet engine is about 150 decibels. A sound level of 163 decibels can shatter a window. The loudest sound a human being can stand is 120 decibels, but anything higher than 85 decibels can be harmful to the human ear.

Give It Your Best Earshot

LEVEL: 1

Strike a pencil on a tabletop. You hear a *thwack*, naturally. Rest one ear on the table. Predict whether the sound of the striking pencil will be louder or softer. Now strike. Were you correct? The sound is louder. The first time you struck the pencil, you heard the sound through the air. The second time, you heard it through the tabletop. Sound travels much faster through solids and liquids than it does through gases, such as air. The table is solid matter.

Did You Know?

If you and a friend were on the moon, you could scream and yell at the top of your lungs, and your friend would not hear you at all. In space, there is no air to vibrate, so there is no sound.

WHAT IS PITCH?

No, it's not what that guy on the mound does during a baseball game. And *perfect pitch* does not necessarily describe a good curveball. Take off that baseball cap, put on your thinking cap, and let's get down to the business of learning about pitch—the *scientific* one.

Wish Me Pluck

LEVEL: 2

You will need:
large rubber band
desk chair

1. Stretch the rubber band over the back of the chair.
2. With your thumb and index finger, grasp the rubber band tightly and stretch it down a little. Use your other hand to pluck the rubber band and make it vibrate.
3. Move your thumb and finger down to make the size of the vibrating section larger. Pluck again. Repeat, making the section larger each time before you pluck.

What happens?
The smaller areas make a higher sound. As the area becomes larger, the sound becomes lower. This is called adjusting the pitch. As the length of vibrating section increases, the pitch decreases.

Why?
Some sounds are higher than others. We say they have a higher pitch. *Pitch* is the number of vibrations per second, or frequency of vibration. The more vibrations per second, the higher the pitch. Smaller objects tend to vibrate faster than larger objects. That's why the smaller sections of rubber band have a higher pitch than the larger ones.

Did You Know?

On a piano, the frequency of middle C is 256 vibrations (cycles) per second, or 256 Hz (hertz). The frequency of high C is 512 Hz. The higher the frequency, the higher the pitch. Next time you are at a piano, look at the metal cords inside. Are they all the same length? Which cords are longer, those above or those below middle C? The bars on a xylophone look the same except for their length. If you strike the different bars, you will find that the shorter bars make the higher sounds. Remember, smaller objects vibrate faster than larger ones.

Strike Up the Can

LEVEL: 1

Strike an empty coffee can with a metal spoon. Now strike an empty soup or juice can with the same spoon. Which can made the higher sound?

HOW CAN AIR BE USED TO MAKE MUSIC?

You've heard clarinet players, saxophone players, and horn players make beautiful sounds and music with their instruments. How do they do this? After all, they're just blowing air.

Pitch-er Perfect

LEVEL: 3

To learn more about the role pitch plays in music, you'll be creating a makeshift flute.

You will need:
at least 4 glasses of the same size and shape, or 4 test tubes (available at science supply stores)
water
food coloring, any color

1. Arrange the glasses in a row about 1 inch apart. Fill the glasses with different amounts of water, starting from least to most; for example, 1 inch, 2 inches, 3 inches, 4 inches. (*Note:* If you are using test tubes, mold some clay into a thick strip and push the rounded ends of the test tubes into it to make them stand up.)
2. Make the water easier to see by adding a drop or two of food coloring to each glass.
3. Blow across the tops of the glasses, one at a time. Which yielded the lowest pitch? Which yielded the highest?

What happens?

The glass with the least amount of water (and the greatest amount of air) has the lowest pitch. The glass with the greatest amount of water (and the least amount of air) has the highest pitch.

Why?

When you blow over the top of each glass, the column of air sitting on top of the water vibrates. The longest column of air produces the lowest pitch. The shortest column of air produces the highest pitch. The amount of water changes the frequency and pitch. The glass with the most water vibrates the most and has the highest pitch. The glass with the least water vibrates the least and has the lowest pitch.

Try This!

Instead of blowing over the glasses, tap them one at a time with a wooden spoon. Now you are making the entire glass vibrate. Does this make a difference in pitch? The glass with the greatest amount of water has the lowest pitch, and the glass with the smallest amount of water has the highest pitch.

Don't Panic!

LEVEL: 3

A panpipe is an ancient musical instrument made of 10 or more tubes or pipes of increasing length. It is named after Pan, the woodland god. According to myth, the music from Pan's pipes caused insanity in those who would listen, hence the term *panic*.

Make panpipes of your own by gathering scissors, 2 drinking straws, a ruler, and tape. Cut one straw in half, using the ruler to make exact measurements. Cut one of the halves into two equal parts. Then take one of those parts and cut it in half. You should have five pieces of different lengths. Make a reed at one end of each piece. First, flatten one end of each piece. Trim each flattened end into a point. Place a strip of tape, sticky side up, on the edge of a tabletop. Arrange the straws in order from shortest to longest, 1 inch apart. Line up the reed ends evenly along the edge of the table. Press another piece of tape, sticky side down, over the reeds and the first strip of tape, creating a "straw sandwich." Blow through your panpipes and compare the sound each straw makes.

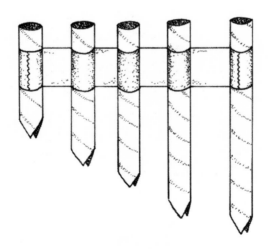

A FINAL NOTE: IS THIS THE END?

As long as there are questions to ask, there won't be an end. A question is a wonderful thing to have, and a great thing to ask. We learn about the world around us by asking questions. Sometimes we find the answers, and sometimes we find new questions to ask.

In this book, we asked a lot of questions about heat, water, air, light, and sound. To find the answers, we performed a variety of experiments using simple materials that you can find in your house or buy at a nearby store. Doing many of these experiments led to some fascinating and surprising answers, and to even more questions.

The most important lesson for you to take away from this book is to keep on asking questions and seeking answers. Remember, if someone asks you a question to which you don't have an answer, don't be embarrassed to say "I don't know." Just follow it with "Let's find out!"

ABOUT THE AUTHOR

Caryl M. Lieberman, M.S. taught science in the New York City public school system for twenty-eight years.

She is a graduate of Barnard College, and received her Master of Science in Education at the City University of New York.